All scriptures are from the King James Version of
The Holy Bible, unless otherwise indicated.

Book Design & Cover by LYNDA MAUPIN
Cover Photo: Red River Gorge- Stanton, Kentucky

Graphic Swirl Headings
Designed and Created
by Emmanuel, my 8 year old son.

Gleaning Handfuls of Purpose

Along the Way...

For More Information Email: *PurposeAlongtheWay@gmail.com*
Website under construction and coming soon...

ISBN 13-978-0615989051
ISBN 10-0615989055
Library of Congress Catalog Card Number: Pending
Printed in the United States of America
©2013 by Lynda Maupin

Along the Way...
Copyright © 2013 by Lynda Maupin

All rights reserved. This book is protected by the copyright laws of the United States of America. No part of this publication may be reproduced, stored in a retrieval system, or transmitted in whole or in part in any form or means- for example, electronic, photocopying, recording, or otherwise, without prior express permission of writer or publisher.

This Book is Dedicated
To my LORD and Savior JESUS The CHRIST.
Thank You LORD for Saving me at a young age, for loving me, keeping me, for the Supernatural Impartations, and for teaching me your ways... a lot more to learn, still GRATEFUL for the Journey, *Along the Way*...
I LOVE YOU LORD!!!!

To my precious, delightful Children who rise up and call me Blessed! You Inspire, Encourage and are a Blessing!!!!
A Gift from GOD

To my Spiritual Parents, Mentors, and "Coach", who sees the Best in every human being. You know who you are.

GOD BLESS You All!!!
I Love you in the LORD!!!

Gleaning Handfuls of Purpose

Along the Way...

A story in a Testimony...
As many Believed...
Received

"Impossible" Can Be Made Possible...
#If U Believe

Lynda Maupin

Thank You LORD!!!!
I am GRATEFUL!!!!

Over a Billion Reasons
To Thank You LORD
For the Love You placed in my Heart
For the Pressing and Blessings in my story
For my thoughts articulated into my words
For Keeping me so that I might have a Testimony
For Your Strength in my journey
Along the Way...

_____*Gift Page*_____

To
_____

From
_____

Date
_____

"Impossible" Can Be Made Possible…
#If U Believe

"And they overcame him by the Blood of the Lamb, and by the word of their Testimony..."

Revelation 12:11

Table of Contents
with some
Correlating Thoughts & Paraphrased Scriptures

Intro of Thoughts & Development of Story Pages 11-29
"No Man is an Island" **11**
"...lo, I Am with you always..."
Matthew 28:20
"Standing in the Gap". **13**
GOD LOVES You!!!
"Only Believe...". **15**
A Story in a Testimony **19**
"We love Him, because He first loved us."
1John 4:19
A Light for My Path **21**
I'm at Home with My Purpose...
on This Side of Heaven **23**
It's Never too Late with the Right
Vision **25**
This Little Book is For YOU... If You Can
Breathe, You Can Achieve More! **29**
"Gonna Be Alright" **31**
Guarded Memories **33**
"...Forgetting those things which are
behind..." Philippians 3:13
"Count it All Joy" **37**

A Sign and a Word of Encouragement. .*39*
Give GOD the Pen, Turn it Over to Him.41
To Give is to Live & Survive Joyfully . . .*43*
Useful Anyhow *45*
Pickings Were Slim *49*
Psalm 91 . . . . *50 & 51*
A New Start *53*
The Commute *55*
"Thank You LORD for Life!"
She Didn't Always Have to Hide
Her Tears *59*
Whatever Comes may... It's Ok *61*
Divine Intervention *67*
It Was a Set Up *71*
I am Who GOD Says I am . . . .*76 & 77*
Breaking Up With Fear *87*
A Sample Collection of Poems & Songs
  Lydia Wrote Along the Way *92-95*
Surrendering *99*
Permission to Prosper *103*
Poems, Songs & Notes of Encouragement
(Reiteration & Journal Thoughts)
Lydia Wrote, Along the Way *114-144*

"Behold, I will do a new thing; now it shall spring forth; shall ye not know it? I will even make a way in the wilderness, and rivers in the desert."

Isaiah 43:19

Along the Way...

"No Man is an Island"

Contrary to what some might think or believe, because of their wilderness experience of obscurity... Seemingly allows them to think that on this planet of 7 billion plus in population, that they are alone. Maybe some do not have family or friends, and they feel as though they must face things in complete solitude. Nevertheless, we do not stand on our own, or alone. GOD is always with us, giving us the posture and the strength to stand strong.

"...Be ye all of one mind, having compassion one of another, love as brethren..."

1 Peter 3:8

Along the Way...

Standing in the Gap

Throughout history GOD has used men and women to do His "Bidding" in the earth. He calls humans into our lives as an extension of His love, utilized to do His work; encouraging thy brethren as ambassadors for Christ. He places people in our lives to stand in the gap. They have been strategically assigned to us, to guide, impart, and intercede on our behalf; i.e. overseers if you will. Adding an extended hand to thy brethren of faith, hope, and "It's not over 'til GOD says it's over."

This story and Testimony exemplifies that... Although you have been on the back side of your desert... Hold on! It's always blindly dark before the *enlightening*, radiant dawn... over the horizon.

"Be strong and of a good courage, fear not, nor be afraid of them: for the LORD thy GOD, He it is that doth go with thee; He will not fail thee, no forsake thee."

Deuteronomy 31:6

"I will lift up mine eyes unto the hills, from whence cometh my help. My help cometh from the LORD, which made heaven and earth."

Psalm 121:1-2

Along the Way...

"Only Believe"

When her courage started dwindling away due to circumstances, detours, and delays. Mediocrity began to place her dreams on hold. The ambers that once burned inside went out without notice. GOD'S Intervention Team stepped in, and encouraged her to believe and hope again, in herself and all that GOD had waiting for her. That which was becoming dormant began to breathe and live again.

This is not a unique Testimony... She's just one in million who can attest to GOD'S love in what some would consider an unlikely place. The word that was for many, seemed to be just for her. She found herself in a midst of counselors guiding her *along the way.*

Gleaning Handfuls of Purpose

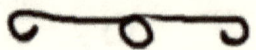

"In all thy ways acknowledge Him, and He shall direct thy paths."

Proverbs 3:6

Along the Way...

A bridge of hope and strength, an extended heart adding strength unto thy brethren, as many Believed.... Received.

GOD'S Intervention on this earth is more than realized and is extremely intentional...

Thank You LORD, for Your love that You dispatch upon the earth!

"Nay, in all these things we are more than conquerors through Him that loved us.

For I am persuaded, that neither death, nor life, nor angels, nor principalities, nor powers, nor things present, nor things to come,

Nor height, nor depth, nor any other creature, shall be able to separate us from the love of GOD, which is in CHRIST JESUS our LORD."
Romans 8:37-39

Along the Way...

A Story in a Testimony

This is a love story, but different than most. GOD'S Divine Intervention in a life that inadvertently gave up on thriving and flourishing, just to survive and exist.

When humans seemingly lose their way and grow weary, it isn't as easy as it would seem, keeping sight of the trail that was intended… GOD and all His sovereignty, knows what we need and when. GOD'S Intervention on this earth is more than realized, and He intentionally utilizes everyday human beings to do His Work… His hands in the earth.

"I will go before thee, and make the crooked places straight: I will break in pieces the gates of brass, and cut in sunder the bars of iron."

Isaiah 45:2

"Thy Word is a lamp unto my feet, and a light unto my path."

Psalm 119:105

Along the Way...

A Light for My Path

Along the Way is a peek into small episodes, of a journey that would have been bleak and less visible, had it not been mined, mapped-out and directed by a riveting, epic, and inspirational dialogue of imparted strength and hope; to believe and begin again. Ushering someone that began to live in less than "normalcy" to the extraordinary. Gaining an understanding of purpose, and an appreciation of saturated wisdom *along the way*.

She triumphantly received new and clear vision; trading in a dusty debris covered path for a brightly lit and clear path in the spiritual... In the form of mentors, teachers and guides, who lead by GOD navigated her safely home.

"Finally, brethren, whatsoever things are true, whatsoever things are honest, whatsoever things are just, whatsoever things are pure, whatsoever things are lovely, whatsoever things are of good report; if there be any virtue, and if there be any praise, think on these things."

Philippians 4:8

Along the Way...

I'm at Home with My Purpose…

On This Side of Heaven

They say that "Home is where the heart is." Well, *earthly* home for Lydia is everything that is viable and purposed for her life, an abundant life full of GOD'S promises.

"Having made known unto us the mystery of His will, according to His good pleasure which He hath purposed in Himself:

That in the dispensation of the fullness of times He might gather together in one all things in CHRIST, both which are in Heaven, and which are on earth; even in Him:

In Whom also we have obtained an inheritance, being predestinated according to the purpose of Him who worketh all things after the council of His own will.
Ephesians 1:9-11

"But without faith it is impossible to please Him: for he that cometh to GOD must believe that He is, and that He is a rewarder of them that diligently seek Him."

Hebrews 11:6

Along the Way...

It's Never Too Late with the Right Vision

In the beginning for some... at least for Lydia, growing up she always believed something good was going to happen. I believe it is then; childhood, when we get our first untainted, full of faith glimpse of our purpose.

Whether we recognize it or not, it is a talent, gifting or an area that we feel the most compassionate about. Oftentimes that childlike faith dissipates, as it is met with a continuous series of unwelcomed and unwarranted blows of disbelief. Just and unjust circumstances i.e. Life just happens.

"Now faith is the substance of things hoped for, the evidence of things not seen."

Hebrews 11:1

Along the Way...

Those rose colored, full of faith glasses, are replaced with scratched, speckled, and blurry bifocals that were somehow meant to help us see things more clearly.

However the harsh realities of disdained lack of vision only allows a distorted sight of spiritual vision. Sending most humans stumbling *along the way.*

In the stumbling, search, and expedition of fulfillment to venture on the right path, many are detoured off track by circumstances and our own choices; unknowingly replacing our GOD given purpose with constant counterfeits of temporary happiness OR becoming haphazardly busy and settling for our current circumstances… putting the pursuit off for "better"… as if "better" will come by osmosis and on its own.

"Before I formed thee in the belly I knew thee; and before thou camest forth out of the womb I sanctified thee, and I ordained thee a prophet unto the nations."

Jeremiah 1:5

"For I know the thoughts that I think toward you, saith the LORD, thoughts of peace, and not of evil, to give you an expected end."

Jeremiah 29:11

"...The race is not to the swift, nor the battle to the strong, neither yet bread to the wise, nor yet riches to men of understanding, nor yet favour to men of skill; but time and chance happeneth to them all."

Ecclesiastes 9:11

"For with GOD nothing shall be impossible."
Luke 1:37

Along the Way...

This story is written for them... For every human being that is walking around aimless, or has even stopped wandering, and has placed their dreams, and purpose on the back burner of a hot plate.

For every person that got distracted, delayed, ventured on the wrong path, and forcefully pushed astray.

Know this: As long as there is still oxygen flowing in and out of your lungs, you can still make a life, and not just a living, by walking into your **GOD GIVEN PUPOSE!**

"And we know that all things work together for good to them that love GOD, to them who are the called according to His purpose."

Romans 8:28

Along the Way...

"I Gotta Feelin' that Everything is Gonna Be Alright!!"

"I gotta feelin' that everything is gonna be alright!" Lydia and her daughter exclaimed simultaneously. This was their song and "motto" of comfort... A song that resonated from the pit of their separate, but connected bellies of a well spring of hope; a song that was sung over and over again in difficult times.

Jubilee, Lydia's ten-year-old daughter smiled and grabbed the rest of her things to take out to the moving truck. Lydia looked at the empty walls and vacant rooms, making sure everything was pristine for whomever gets the house that they lost through foreclosure.

"...For the joy of the LORD is your strength."

Nehemiah 8:10

Along the Way...

Guarded Memories...

As Lydia looks around she is caught off guard by the laughter that echoes in her ears, as she reflects over the memories that took place during the years. While glancing over at the staircase, she remembers her children sliding down the stairs between her legs before she could make it down. Then quickly replaces a not so cheerful memory with a joyful one of her nursing her son... *while sitting on the window seal of the newly framed house, a fresh breeze flows through all the open walls, windows, and doors. Providing just enough structure for privacy and comfort...* She quickly collects herself and her memories while walking to the front door to exit

that house for the last time...

"And it shall be, when the LORD thy GOD shall have brought thee into the land which He sware unto thy fathers, to Abraham, to Isaac, and to Jacob, to give thee great and goodly cities, which thou buildedst not, And houses full of all good things, which thou filledst not, and wells digged, which thou diggedst not, vineyards and olive trees, which thou plantedst not; when thou shalt have eaten and be full."

Deuteronomy 6:10-11

Along the Way...

She holds her arms up in the air in Praise and Thanksgiving to GOD, for ever having the opportunity to have a house.

"This is the day which the LORD hath made; we will rejoice and be glad in it."

Psalm 118:24

"Rejoice in the LORD always: and again I say, Rejoice."

Philippians 4:4

Along the Way...

"Count it All Joy"

Lydia, Jubilee, and her six-year-old son Josiah, do their best to create a home. Uniquely using her ability to improvise in the confines of a very small apartment.

Lydia actually had an unlikely excitement to improvise and make their new place of living; as nice as she could for her children... Her children were excited as well; improvising her immaculate skills of survival on less... As if she was reliving her childhood fantasy of *being trapped on a desolate island; learning and surviving on an extremely limited terrain.*

"We are troubled on every side, yet not distressed; we are perplexed, but not in despair; Persecuted, but not forsaken; cast down, but not destroyed;"
2 Corinthians 4:8-9

"For though we walk in the flesh, we do not war after the flesh (For the weapons of our warfare are not carnal, but mighty through GOD to the pulling down of strong holds) Casting down imaginations, and every high thing that exalteth itself against the knowledge of GOD, and bringing into captivity every thought to the obedience of Christ;"

2 Corinthians 10:3-5

Along the Way...

A Sign and a Word of Encouragement

Starting over again financially and somewhat mentally was extremely difficult at times for Lydia, and only seemed to get worse.

After selling most of what was left of their household belongings from the previous house to provide some sort of income... Driving "home" one evening after a very discouraging day of uncertainty. At a momentary point of extreme desperation, rivers of tears flowed from Lydia's eyes as the radio's volume in the back-ground played low. Suddenly the radio's pitch ignited as a minister began to speak. "You ever seen a deer when it takes off?...Well that's how your life is going to take off!"

"But they that wait upon the LORD
shall renew their strength; they shall mount
up with wings as eagles; they shall run, and
not be weary; and they shall walk,
and not faint."
Isaiah 40:31

"My brethren, count it all joy when ye fall into divers temptations; Knowing this, that the trying of your faith worketh patience. But let patience have her perfect work, that ye may be perfect and entire, wanting nothing."
James 1:2-4

"Now thanks be unto GOD, which always causeth us to triumph in CHRIST, and maketh manifest the Savior of His knowledge by us in every place."
2 Corinthians 2:14

Along the Way...

Give GOD the Pen ...Turn it over to Him
Let Him Write the Story of your Life.

At that very moment, with a gazed and teary eyed stare... As the word on the radio program penetrated her very being. A huge deer briefly pauses in front of her car and takes off suddenly and simultaneously to the word that is given over the radio!!!

In the midst of desperation and severe testing... "Divers temptation"... In moments of uncertainty, and a night full of tears... within moments, turned into joy; miraculous *signs and wonders* of confirmation; that no matter how bleak things seemed to be... GOD who had Never let her down; was going to write the rest of her story, no need to worry... And not only was GOD going before her, but all at this very moment was well...

"...It is more blessed to give than to receive."

Acts 20:35

"Thou shalt love thy neighbour as thyself. There is none other commandment greater than these."

Mark 12:31

Along the Way...

To Give is to Live...

As Lydia walks in to the store to get some supplies needed for her family, with the intention to stick to the strict budget of five dollars. She noticed a middle aged lady sitting on the curb. Lydia says "Hi", and somehow that strikes up a conversation. Lydia learns that the woman needs groceries, so she writes a list, with the woman dictating what she would like to have.

Twenty minutes later Lydia comes back to the Dollar Tree to give the lady her few bags of groceries and a hot meal customized to the lady's specifications. Lydia prays with her and before she could leave her presence, the lady quickly asks for a hug.

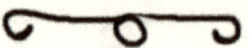

"And the King shall answer and say unto them, Verily I say unto you, Inasmuch as ye have done it unto one of the least of these my brethren, ye have done it unto Me."

Matthew 25:40

Along the Way...

Useful Anyhow

Throughout her life, Lydia has always been grateful to GOD, for Him using her to help others, to be a blessing... giving out of abundance, and now still giving, but out of lack. Caring for others by means of buying a meal, and herself doing without one so she could help someone else, actually blessed her more than the one receiving. GOD provided countless opportunities for His love to shine in random acts of kindness. While sustaining her, and giving much purpose to Lydia. It was as if giving gave Lydia breath to live. She continued to sow... giving what she had. Although circumstances sometimes made her cry on the inside. She never lost her witness on the outside... Gratefully caring for those she believed GOD placed in her path with joy.

Along the Way...

"Blessed are the poor in spirit: for theirs is the kingdom of heaven.

Blessed are they that mourn: for they shall be comforted.

Blessed are the meek: for they shall inherit the earth.

Blessed are they which do hunger and thirst after righteousness: for they shall be filled.

Blessed are the merciful: for they shall obtain mercy.

Blessed are the pure in heart: for they shall see GOD.

Blessed are the peacemakers: for they shall be called the children of GOD.

Blessed are they which are persecuted for righteousness' sake: for theirs is the kingdom of heaven."

Matthew 5:3-10

"...Yet have I not seen the righteous forsaken, nor his seed begging bread."
Psalm 37:25

"But my GOD shall supply all your need according to His riches in glory by CHRIST JESUS."
Philippians 4:19

Along the Way...

Pickings Were Slim

As things seemed to get harder she continued to keep her faith and integrity of moral values. When discerned subtle situations of dishonesty or compromise. There was never a question to wait on GOD, and to have a job of respectability without the status quo of hidden agendas. Although Lydia was not perfect, she tried hard to please GOD.

Psalm 91

"He that dwelleth in the secret place of the most High shall abide under the shadow of the Almighty.

²I will say of the LORD, He is my refuge and my fortress: my GOD; in Him will I trust.

³Surely He shall deliver thee from the snare of the fowler, and from the noisome pestilence.

⁴He shall cover thee with His feathers, and under His wings shalt thou trust: His truth shall be thy shield and buckler.

⁵Thou shalt not be afraid for the terror by night; nor for the arrow that flieth by day;

⁶Nor for the pestilence that walketh in darkness; nor for the destruction that wasteth at noonday.

⁷A thousand shall fall at thy side, and ten thousand at thy right hand; but it shall not come nigh thee.

⁸Only with thine eyes shalt thou behold and see the reward of the wicked."

Along the Way...

⁹Because thou hast made the LORD, *which is my refuge, even the most High, thy habitation;*

¹⁰There shall no evil befall thee, neither shall any plague come nigh thy dwelling.

¹¹For He shall give His angels charge over thee, to keep thee in all thy ways.

¹²They shall bear thee up in their hands, lest thou dash thy foot against a stone.

¹³Thou shalt tread upon the lion and adder: the young lion and the dragon shalt thou trample under feet.

¹⁴Because he hath set his love upon Me, therefore will I deliver him: I will set him on high, because he hath known My name.

¹⁵He shall call upon Me, and I will answer him: I will be with him in trouble; I will deliver him, and honour him.

¹⁶With long life will I satisfy him, and shew him My salvation."

Gleaning Handfuls of Purpose

Along the Way...

A New Start?

Finally an early morning phone call for a job offer welcomed her ears to amazement. The job only paid minimum wage. However it was exactly what she needed to be able to accommodate her children's schedule as a single mom. She was thrilled and considered it a blessing.

"But as for you, ye thought evil against me; but GOD meant it unto good, to bring to pass, as it is this day, to save much people alive."

Genesis 50:20

"If it had not been the LORD who was on our side..."

Psalm 124:1

Along the Way...

The Commute

"Thank You LORD For Life!"

In route one morning, anticipating a busy productive day... As Lydia drove on a one way street... A massive truck plummets into her small '97 Corolla! It was a miracle that she was alive!

Her car was totaled, nonetheless she was very thankful that her life was spared. A little bruised up, in extreme pain, and in a neck brace. She went home from the hospital to begin to heal. Unfortunately her back and leg became progressively worse.

"No weapon that is formed against thee shall prosper; and every tongue that shall rise against thee in judgment thou shalt condemn. This is the heritage of the servants of the LORD, and their righteousness is of Me, saith the LORD."

Isaiah 54:17

Along the Way...

After a visit to the hospital, she learns the excruciating pain she endures is caused by sciatic nerve damage and extreme inflammation.

Lydia has no idea that during the next 7 months, that she would experience constant and almost unbearable pain, which inevitably is accompanied with stress. Feeling as though there were *ton pound* weights on her shoulders, emotionally and physically, that she must lift and press against in order to regain the capacity to be viable and fruitful again.

"...Weeping may endure for a night, but joy cometh in the morning."

Psalm 30:5

"For the LORD GOD will help me; therefore shall I not be confounded: therefore have I set my face like a flint, and I know that I shall not be ashamed."

Isaiah 50:7

Along the Way...

She Didn't Always Have to Hide Her Tears

Whenever her youngest son saw her crying, a time or two... Whether it was the pain from her injuries, or the pain from her presumably now *unproductive* life. Lydia's rehearsed and received response brought much satisfaction and joy to her son. She would smile while tears rolled down her cheeks and simply say, "I'm getting rid of the extra tears to make room for the Exceeding Joy!"

That beautiful strength from the LORD, was a foundation of liquid steel, poured and being instilled... GOD was continuously setting the *footing* for their portion of strength and joy to face the days ahead.

"But He was wounded for our transgressions, He was bruised for our iniquities: the chastisement of our peace was upon Him; and with His stripes we are healed."

Isaiah 53:5

"And I will restore to you the years that the locust hath eaten, the cankerworm, and the caterpillar, and the palmerworm, my great army which I sent among you."

Joel 2:25

Along the Way...

What Ever Comes May... It's Okay

As the days went by... Lydia's debilitating pain progressed, keeping her house bound and in bed most of the day. So not only was she dealing with various health issues from the car accident, but she didn't have health insurance.

Her strength in her body, and her previous tenacious, not settling attitude began to disintegrate. The act of doing was becoming less, and the ritual of not doing was becoming more. The more her circumstance continued to exude a poignant stench of disappointment, the more she began to lower her expectations. If not consciously...subconsciously.

"Behold, I will do a new thing; now it shall spring forth; shall ye not know it? I will even make a way in the wilderness, and rivers in the desert."

Isaiah 43:19

Along the Way...

This enabled her to somewhat survive mentally on a lower amount of pain; becoming comfortable with what would normally have been uncomfortable to this once extremely motivated and energetic lady...

As to resemble to be a "sell out"…with notions of not being able to change her circumstance. She placed her dreams on layaway, as if she could save up enough "change" to one day try and invest in life again, when everything was favorable. Almost comfortable with being mediocre, but what would be surprising to most, she still somehow found a way to make the best out of the situation, *in her eyes*. She remained grateful and made herself content, realizing there were people on this planet that overcame greater circumstances than this.

*"That if thou shalt confess with thy mouth the
LORD JESUS, and shalt believe in thine heart
that GOD hath raised Him from the dead,
thou shalt be saved. For with the heart
man believeth unto righteousness;
and with the mouth confession is
made unto salvation."*

Romans 10:9-10

*"For GOD so loved the world,
that He gave His only begotten Son,
that whosoever believeth in Him
should not perish, but
have everlasting life."
John 3:16*

Along the Way...

So while temporarily "things" may have been less than desirable at times, Lydia and her children were grateful and very thankful for much!

Especially for Salvation! Their belief, faith, and personal relationship with GOD, was carrying them through.

"For our light affliction, which is but for a moment, worketh for us a far more exceeding and eternal weight of glory;

While we look not at the things which are seen, but at the things which are not seen: for the things which are seen are temporal; but the things which are not seen are eternal."
2 Corinthians 4:17-18

*"Being confident of this very thing,

that He which hath begun a good work in you

will perform it until the day of JESUS CHRIST."*

Philippians 1:6

Along the Way...

Divine Intervention

Although Lydia didn't own or have access to a computer, she owned a small phone that had Internet access. While searching for some sort of income prospect, maybe a job she could do from home that would accommodate her condition of almost constant pain, and limited mobility. She stumbled up on one of her favorite Pastor's Facebook page information, so she logged on and unbeknownst to her this was the beginning to a conversation that would forever change her life through an unlikely place… the Internet. She gained a different "take" on the social media scene.

The Great Commission

"Then the eleven disciples went away into Galilee, into a mountain where JESUS had appointed them.

And when they saw Him, they worshipped Him: but some doubted.

And JESUS came and spake unto them, saying, "All power is given unto Me in heaven and in earth.

Go ye therefore, and teach all nations, baptizing them in the name of the Father, and of the Son, and of the Holy Ghost:

Teaching them to observe all things whatsoever I have commanded you: and, lo, I Am with you always, even unto the end of the world. Amen."

Matthew 28:16-20

Along the Way...

What many view as secular... had been infiltrated and saturated by the "Great Commission" i.e. The Encouraging Word of GOD. She began to interact with people she had never met... And most relevant to this story, a group of Global Ministers, Leaders, and Inspirational people on Facebook and Twitter; who she grew to think of as, "GOD'S Intervention Team."

"So shall My word be that goeth forth out of My mouth: it shall not return unto Me void, but it shall accomplish that which I please, and it shall prosper in the thing whereto I sent it."

Isaiah 55:11

Along the Way...

It Was a Set Up

Gleaning handfuls of purpose *along the way*

The word that was for many, seemed to be just for her. Each time she read their status updates, it was as if they were customized just for her particular situation.

They say that there are no coincidences in life; this was the supporting example of that ideology. Their words of encouragement far surpassed her expectations from day to day. They had a willingness to teach, she had a willingness to learn. She found herself in the midst of counselors guiding her *along the way.*

"By this shall all men know that ye are My disciples, if ye have love one to another."

John 13:35

Along the Way...

A bridge of hope and courage; an extended heart adding strength unto thy brethren; as many believed, received. Their yielded vessels to GOD were an extension of His hands throughout the land. Their collaborated efforts of hope and love stood in the gap for many.

What an amazing voyage this was for Lydia. Part of the joy in her that kept her going was her love for her children and others. It truly brought joy to see other's victories and successes... Although it appeared as though she didn't equate her own self in the same sense. It seemed that she didn't think she needed to go any further...as far as all those hopes and dreams, still on the back burner of that hot plate that had turned cold.

"(As it is written, I have made thee a father of many nations), before Him whom he believed, even GOD, who quickeneth the dead, and calleth those things which be not as though they were."
Romans 4:17

"For verily I say unto you, That whosoever shall say unto this mountain, Be thou removed, and be thou cast into the sea; and shall not doubt in his heart, but shall believe that those things which he saith shall come to pass; he shall have whatsoever he saith. Therefore I say unto you what things soever ye desire, when ye pray, believe that ye receive them, and ye shall have them."
Mark 11:23-24

"For as he thinketh in his heart, so is he..."
Proverbs 23:7

Along the Way...

Surprisingly she posted on Twitter and Facebook about success as if she already was successful. Helping others online and off by what she deemed as insignificant acts of kindness. At the time she felt the most depleted, and thought she possessed the least to give, was the time that she became the most useful. While she gleaned handfuls of purpose, she also used what was gathered from her journey *along the way* to feed others.

They say whatever you are starts from the inside out... She was already successful, for it had manifested inside her, and was apparent in her tweets. You definitely can't judge a book by its cover, because the cover was already a success. While her contents were just getting revamped, edited, and rewritten.

Truth is revealed in many ways, and very beneficial in the long run.

Knowledge allows understanding...

Take what you have learned in the past... and quickly apply it to recollection.

When walking in purpose and on purpose, I must not only know where

I am going, but who is going...

I am fearfully and wonderfully made... (Psalm 139:14)

I am above only and not beneath... (Deuteronomy 28:13)

I am a joint-heir with CHRIST (Romans 8:17)

I am more than a conqueror through Him who loves me. (Romans 8:37)

Along the Way...

*I am an ambassador for CHRIST
(2 Corinthians 5:20)*

*I am firmly rooted, built up, established in my faith and overflowing with gratitude
(Colossians 2:7)*

*I am part of a chosen generation, a royal priesthood, a holy nation, a peculiar people
(1 Peter 2:9)*

*I am an overcomer by the Blood of the Lamb and the word of my Testimony
(Revelation 12:11)*

*I am a partaker of His divine nature
(2 Peter 1:3, 4)*

I am a Proverbs 31 Woman

I am who GOD says I am,

nothing more and nothing less...

*Paraphrased

"Let this mind be in you, which was also in CHRIST JESUS!"
Philippians 2:5

"And be not conformed to this world: but be ye transformed by the renewing of your mind, that ye may prove what is that good, and acceptable, and perfect, will of GOD."
Romans 12:2

Along the Way...

She was getting better and better every day, by her encounters *along the way*; unaware that she was finding wealth in a broke and depleted place. A pilgrimage of spiritual manna supplied daily. Every day brought unexpected encounters of wisdom, guidance, and yes, love filled reproach that began to permeate and direct her thinking.

She was reminded that there was more for her than just to exist hand to mouth. This woman who some, because of her financially depleted status, and circumstances, would consider the least. Not to mention she wasn't getting any younger (at least not by chronological standards)… Most would say it was over for her, and that there was no chance for her to turn it around. *However there is a "But GOD" In the midst of every Circumstance and situation.*

"So then neither is he that planteth any thing, neither he that watereth; but GOD that giveth the increase."

1 Corinthians 3:7

Along the Way...

In all actuality she was yet to begin. GOD sent this dialogue of Divine Intervention just in the nick of time... "Weeping may endure for a night, but joy cometh in the morning." Psalms 30:5 Enduring tears would allow her to reap joy. Disappointed tears would become content tears. The trials in her life were becoming priceless lessons of blessings.

During the process of self-discovery she began to realize that settling was selfish. There were people who were waiting for her vessel to be yielded in all that GOD placed in her, so it could get out to others. GOD has invested much.

These "mentors" as she also referred to them, challenged her to step into all that GOD had waiting for her...

*"For My thoughts are not your thoughts,
neither are your ways My ways,
saith the LORD."*

*"For as the heavens are higher than the earth,
so are My ways higher than your ways, and
My thoughts than your thoughts."
Isaiah 55:8-9*

*"Stand therefore, having your loins girt about with
truth, and having on the breastplate of righteousness;
And your feet shod with the preparation
of the gospel of peace;"
Ephesians 6:14, 15*

*"He hath made everything beautiful
in His time."
Ecclesiastics 3:11*

Along the Way...

Not only did they see her potential, but also they saw her current value. For those of us that were perceived the least of these, you esteemed, made use of, and considered great.

Now this was not an easy process by any means. As a matter of fact if you could probe into her most private inner thoughts, you would know there were times she was fighting with every bit of spiritual equipment she had, to occupy.

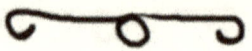

"*Pray without ceasing.*"

1 Thessalonians 5:17

"*For we walk by faith, not by sight.*"

2 Corinthians 5:7

"*Watch ye, stand fast in the faith, quit you like men, be strong!*"

1 Corinthians 16:13

"*...I humbled my soul with fasting and my prayer returned into mine own bosom.*"

Psalm 35:13

Along the Way...

A very excruciating shift occurred with every new discovery. Her faith in GOD and His word would never falter her, nor did she let go and falter it. Faith kept her in every aspect of the word "kept".

"Now unto Him that is able to keep you from falling, and to present you faultless before the presence of His glory with exceeding joy..."
Jude 1:24

"For by grace are ye Saved through faith; and that not of yourselves: it is the gift of GOD:
Not of works lest any man should boast."
Ephesians 2:8-9

"For GOD hath not given us the spirit of fear; but of power, and of love, and of a sound mind."

2 Timothy 1:7

Along the Way...

Breaking Up With Fear

During her journey she discovered a "Goliath" of fear, if you will. He came in unannounced and uninvited. When she finally noticed him in her abode, she asked him... while pondering her thoughts, "How did you get in?!" and surprisingly he answered... All of the sudden her thoughts were inundated with occurrences and points of entry. Once she recognized his introduction, she recalled countless harassing taunts of bullying, she quickly realized that she had already gained ground and began to end the "bittersweet" relationship that was never consummated.

"Be strong and of a good courage, fear not, nor be afraid of them: for the LORD thy GOD, He it is that doth go with thee; He will not fail thee, nor forsake thee."

Deuteronomy 31:6

Along the Way...

As a matter of fact, when she logged into the Internet and began communicating on social media, she realized she had already served (fear) notice, that she was no longer going to tolerate him (fear) dropping in whenever he (fear) pleased. You see, Lydia used to have a fear of the Internet. She stayed away from computers for approximately twelve years.

How amazing it is, and can be, if something that presents its self as a problem or fear is overcome, unraveled and faced…There can be a blessing within. It was almost as if "the opposers of progress" saw the deliverance in her future that would come about through modern technology, via social media… and put up road blocks of fear prior, hoping they would not be removed; knowing what would manifest if she pressed.

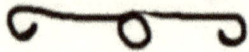

"But as it is written, eye hath not see, nor ear heard, neither have entered into the heart of man, the things which GOD hath prepared for them that love Him."

1 Corinthians 2:9

Along the Way...

Nevertheless, pressed is what she did. Fighting to regain her bearings against insurmountable odds, pushing past the roadblocks and debris of fear to live again!!!

"Brethren, I count not myself to have apprehended: but this one thing I do, forgetting those things which are behind, and reaching forth unto those things which are before, I press toward the mark for the prize of the high calling of GOD in CHRIST JESUS."
Philippians 3:13-14

Transitioning

I thought transition was supposed to be easy…
Have I been in this place too long?

Most people probably don't understand…
I didn't either before these circumstances began.

I understand now the hurt and the pain of trying,
hoping, and believing again…

The people that others walk over or don't notice…
The homeless or dormant or settling for less…
Are people who gave up and gave in to life's stress.

I thank GOD that I always sympathized and helped… and now I empathize and wish I could help.

I am crying out loud… but silently…
Praying to GOD to enable me.

I hear in my spirit… this is not as hard as I think,
Just transitioning from process to progress…

There but by the Grace of GOD go all of us…

Along the Way...

This has been desert scorched, but not parched, and thirst quenched... A wilderness of obscurity and abandonment, but not alone... Weak and weary, but strong and strengthened... sometimes empty, yet filled and nourished... A pilgrimage of uncertainty, yet learning and answers given... pungent pressing, from the crushing as an olive, yet refined, being restored and better than before... to the putting back together the many broken pieces and being shaped on the Potter's wheel... transitioning into a new dimension of existence... Increased by the LORD.

THANK YOU JESUS!!!!

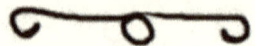

I know there is a miracle in this… because there is so much pain in the birthing process…

Giving up is easy… continuing to push is hard…

Today in all its extremities I realized I have to do things differently….

I have to breathe in between…

I've never gone through so much agony in such a short time…

Sometimes when I just exist it's more bearable than to try.

This has to be labor… because when I don't push, I have the feeling that there is something GOD placed in me… that if I don't get it out it won't survive.

Along the Way...

"You can make it out if you just don't quit."

Break through barriers and uncertainty

Through mundane habits of dormancy

Lack of real productivity

To gain the inclination not to remain

But to make a change

Must press to be actual and factual

Not words without action

To press to push and to stretch

Until effort and effectiveness

Becomes a habit of improving

Is success.

Along the Way...

Fighting hard through the limitations of stagnation and monotonous visits, with subtle threats of reclusiveness.

There was and is more purpose to this than I could have ever imagined...
It is a pulling... and a pressing; beyond pain; strain; and fear...
A once regularly used effort... to train to exert force and motion again...

Dormancy is an awful place to be. Once there everything becomes non-progressive and non-productive...

During this voyage, not only did Lydia gather a more pronounced and vigilant way of thinking... She realized that Dormancy is a place that is difficult to leave once you've moved in... and you don't realize your there until you have fully unpacked most of the vigilance, tenacity and fight and taken up occupancy. Therefore continuing to stay relevant; viable; functional; and limber... Staying as active as possible is a very important workout that should never end. There is an old adage... "If you don't use it, you lose it." Do everything unto the Glory of GOD, and GOD will always make your "little" Much!

"And Jabez called on the GOD of Israel, saying, Oh that thou wouldest bless me indeed, and enlarge my coast, and that thine hand might be with me, and that thou wouldest keep me from evil, that it may not grieve me! And GOD granted him that which he requested."

1 Chronicles 4:10

Along the Way...

Surrendering

Surrendering to the process of self-discovery; allowing GOD to stretch her was a mental workout that Lydia would never forget.

In these daily conversations over the wireless Internet frequencies, she felt accountability to people who may not even know she existed. It was amazing, through this pilgrimage *along the way*, she acquired a new passion and gifts, that were stirred up and cultivated by this dialogue, and communicating her thoughts on her journey. She recaptured her vision; new gifts and ideas began to flow and catapult.

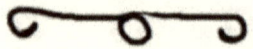

"But we have this treasure in earthen vessels,

that the excellency of the power

may be of GOD, and not of us."

2 Corinthians 4:7

Along the Way...

This may bring a bit of humor to your mind's eye… If you had sight of what was going on in the inside of her, you would see a human form with what looks like a blender on high speed inside of her. The gifts were being stirred up and multiplying.

Her desire to help others and her family was greater… than her desire to relinquish the progress and quit… Change became imminent. She began to understand that purpose cannot be put on hold or on "layaway". It is a progressive effort of steps, no matter how small.

"Now unto Him that is able to do exceeding abundantly above all that we ask or think, according to the power that worketh in us."

Ephesians 3:20

*"...Looking unto JESUS
The Author and Finisher of our faith..."
Hebrews 12:2*

Along the Way...

Permission to Prosper

One day Lydia heard a small and still voice in her mind say, "Will thou have an abundant life?" She expeditiously but quietly whispered, "Yes I will..."

Called away from the familiar into a productive land; she transitioned from the realm of lack and "failure" into an area of abundance and success!

Now instead of just letting life happen to her, she decided to happen to life. Realizing that circumstances and situations cannot dictate her life, or write her story, but only promote it! She began to write her story and Testimony. Anticipating and in great expectation for the next door of opportunity! ...

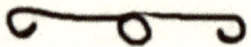

"...I will give thee the treasures of darkness, and hidden riches of secret places, that thou mayest know that I, the LORD, which call thee by thy name, am the GOD of Israel."

Isaiah 45:3

Along the Way...

It is absolutely amazing...

GOD'S sovereignty, all powerful and mystical work of turning and using all things for our good! While so much decreased materially, her wisdom and understanding increased... through her mistakes, blunders, detours, circumstance, and heartbreak. She stumbled upon heart builders, not heart breakers. Propelling her into her purpose and destiny. In life while we see undesirable occurrences as hindrances, distractions and delays... they are only indicators that **Blessings are on the way...**

OH and did I tell you that The LORD Healed Lydia's body!!!! GLORY HALLELUJAH!!!! Now she's really ready to run on...with not just Exuberance, but with unquenched and unhindered stamina in the Spirit and in the natural... "Running on to see what the ends gonna be..." **BLESSED BE THE NAME OF THE LORD!!!!!!!!!!!!!!!!**

Comments from the Author...

Like any story... after it's been lived... When it's communicated verbally or expressed on paper... Many details and major events are left out... As in life, it would be very lengthy to describe in It's entirety. This is the shorter version of one of *Lydia's Testimonies... along the way*. A **more detailed** version, as well as more of Lydia's Series of Short Stories, and other books **will be *coming soon...***

Thank you so much for reading.

GOD Bless you!

Along the Way...

"Working For Our Good"

It was a Divine, Orchestrated, Intentional Dialogue and labor of love.

It was a set up!!!!

"I am the vine, ye are the branches: He that abideth in Me, and I in him, the same bringeth forth much fruit: for without Me ye can do nothing."
John 15:5

"Without counsel purposes are disappointed: but in the multitude of counsellors they are established."
Proverbs 15:2

Along the Way…

To GOD Be the Glory for What He Has Done!

"Being confident of this very thing, that He which hath begun a good work in you will perform it until the day of JESUS CHRIST." Philippians 1:6

I am Grateful LORD for what You are doing in and With me!!!! THANK YOU LORD SO MUCH!!!!

"…Honor to whom honor is due." Romans 13:7
To my Spiritual Parents and Mentors
I give honor to you!!! **You make a difference!**

You have blessed my life… To try again and to finish something I've started has already made me a success and I'm in a Spiritually wealthy place.

I humbly and sincerely submit this Testimony/Story
Thank you for leaving *Extra* on Purpose…
   "Nothing Wasted"

Along the Way...

"Bring ye all the tithes into the storehouse, that there may be meat in Mine house, and prove Me now herewith, saith the LORD of hosts, if I will not open you the windows of heaven, and pour you out a blessing, that there shall not be room enough to receive it."

Malachi 3:10

A Little Note of Appreciation to my Mentors:

"Remain Relevant"

I very much appreciate wisdom and Revelation Knowledge and oftentimes I take side notes...

"Remaining Relevant" This and all Postings have been a Wealth of Blessings and understandings *along the way...*

As I thought about it and I referred to these two words...I knew what the words meant. However I needed further exploration on how they should be taken and applied to my life. So I looked in the dictionary... and it read: "Remaining relevant" is, "Bearing upon or connected with the matter in hand." Then I glanced at the word in the dictionary that came before it, which was "relentless"..."unyielding and harsh" Then I looked at the word that came after relevant, which is "reliable", "trust; that can be depended on"...Furthermore the meaning of the words before and after the word relevant; and putting together those surrounding words... means that I must be unyielding, relentless, staying connected to the matter at hand, committed, and dependable to see it through. Amen

    Thank you!!!

Along the Way...

Thank You!!!!
Strengthening me...

Foundation
There is a work that is being done.
A work that no one will see with the naked eye,
It is a work beneath the skin... a work within.
Underground
Underneath
Lies progress in the making
A great awakening
A transformation
Not an outward illustration
Not a billboard sign
But a learning and learned time
Beyond the natural sight
Deep within
I'm getting my second wind...

Writing the book...
There is a process
an experience
that educates
and liberates,
Seeing the groundwork,
the excavation and
building of the structure,
is so valuable,
hard and difficult
but so valuable
Some experiences are worth it all.

Sometimes when I cannot see clearly…

I close my eyes and look through my heart…

Inside there…
is Love and all the things

I hoped for.

The beauty of this world… still exist in there.
If you look hard enough, you will see
all the splendor…

It's grandeur than our eyes can
fathom or perceive…

Close your eyes and look through your heart.

Along the Way...

"Peculiar People"

Be who GOD called you to be, and not what the world wants to see…

Please don't let anyone change you…

GOD made you unique on purpose.

GOD predetermined you.

Every hair, every dimple, every mole, and every wrinkle
is in His plan
not done by man.

You see GOD has called you out of darkness into
the marvelous light.

He wants you to be different and set apart…

I know there will be those who bully and ridicule you,
but you keep standing and doing what's right.

For it is His Son, Who is the only one,
we give our highest account to.

So with all your quirky ways
idiosyncrasies and a mind like a maze.

You will not fit in or blend in.
GOD has called you
to be
different.

.

My strength
comes from the LORD
This Joy that I have…
Is as far as the East is from the West…
It bellows from the North and the South…
It cascades through the valleys and the peaks.
It burst through the clouds from whence it came…
I will never be the same…
This Joy that I have.

"They that sow in tears shall reap in Joy." Psalm 126: 5-6

Being transparent isn't always easy or appealing.
Sharing hardships and circumstance…
There is always a chance people will look at you differently.
I wrote myself a note one day sitting in church.
It read, "GOD wants you to be completely transparent."
And within myself I understood what that meant.
Allowing people to peak into my life, my heart, and my thoughts, is somewhat difficult; and reliving events is as well. Nonetheless without confession and exposure of one's journey, there would be no Testimony…
And an example; that if one human being can get through some of life's *unpleasantries*, so can you.
Because GOD is no respecter of persons… What He will do for one, He will do for you. Acts 10:34
When we share what we've endured and overcome candidly, it adds strength unto thine brethren. That we are not alone in our plights to press and fight on in our journey.
There are many obstacles we face *along the way…*
But with GOD we do not face them alone.

Along the Way...

Keep Going, *Along the Way...*
GOD is My Vehicle

Maybe the road is extremely tough and the pavement has turned rocky and rough...
The signs are hard to see, which ones lead to my destiny...

He said He will never lead me astray,
and that He will keep me
On the narrow and straight...

I have been rerouted, detoured, and seemingly delayed.
But He said I'm right on time and not too late...
He says He will keep me in all His ways...

There may be a lot of bumps in the road *along the way...*
The steering is hard to control...
The potholes keep trying to stop me...

I think I'm running out of gas...
But GOD has assured me this too shall come to pass
"My Word is true and will last"

He will never leave me nor forsake me
He will carry me the rest of the way...
Arriving safely at my destination.

Destiny awaits...

HUMAN
I Love you

My Neighbor on this earth…

You have Great Worth

It's not because your poor or rich

It's simply because you exist

Not because your kind

Not because you smiled

You are GOD'S child
Not because you helped me load my groceries in the line

And not because you're handsome or pretty

For it is your heart that distinguishes your appearance

GOD created you to love and to be loved
My brother or Sister in CHRIST

My Neighbor on this earth…

GOD predestined your birth

You have Great Worth!

GOD Loves you!

Along the Way...

Success ...In the Spiritual and Natural

For generations to come...

I have to remind myself of what JESUS has done,

All the wealth that has been given unto me.

GOD set me free from shame and from
Ever embarking upon a low self-esteem.

I'm not in the realm of doing less

but in an arena of GOD'S Best

Yes He is adding unto me,

Extreme wealth,

A Legacy...

I cried this morning…

My tears are for all the years of uncertainty

All the years of lessons

All the years of Blessings

All the years of lack, and all the years of plenty…

In all the years of less that is when GOD still used me to bless…
and taught me to receive.

In all the years of plenty GOD made me a giver to many…
and increased my capacity to dream.

I cried this morning for all the wealth of endurance, peace,
patience, wisdom, and strength to continue on…

For the Love of the LORD…

For a Jubilant heart in my song,

And for the Joy in my tears

Throughout the years.

Thank You LORD!!!!

Along the Way...

"Now the GOD of hope fill you with all joy and peace in believing, that ye may abound in hope..." Romans 15:13

Circumstances and situations may not have changed, and things may seem to remain the same. However the GOD I serve changes not, and is the same a thousand years ago, today, and every single day thereafter, in the future... Has All Power in His Hands; the ability to change situations in less time than it takes us to blink an eye...

You thought you were off course and delayed. Nevertheless, GOD has the all ability to fast forward your life in such a way that you arrive right on time. All the things you went through, survived and endured, was just Boot camp; equipping you to help someone else through their wilderness experience... Gleaning wisdoms you needed, so that when you started walking into your "Promised Land" (purpose), you would know what to do with it; appreciate it; and occupy it with longevity... Allowing you new understandings of someone else's plight... knowing more than just sympathy, but also empathy...

If you must cry while your being pruned, rejoice also... knowing, If GOD said it that settles it! It Shall come to pass! Now is the time to rejoice!!! *2 Corinthians 1:20 says... "For all the promises of GOD in Him are yea, and in Him Amen, unto the glory of GOD by us." And Ephesians 3:20 says... "Now unto Him that is able to do Exceeding abundantly above all that we ask or think, according to the power that worketh in us..."*

*"Looking towards the hills from whence cometh my help
my help, cometh from the LORD,
which made heaven and earth." Psalm 121:1, 2*

May 19, 2012

On this journey of life…
The path becomes more visible, viable, and valuable.
The road becomes a little straighter, steadier, and smooth.
With GOD
Disappointed tears become content tears,
Hurt tears become healed,
Scared tears become courageous tears
The sorrow becomes unspeakable joy.
The sadness becomes hope.
The pain becomes more bearable.
The anxiousness becomes patient.
The bitterness becomes forgiven.
The fear becomes courage.
The mirage of *failure* becomes Victory Realized.

Along the Way...

Beloved...No doubt, But Faith and Assurance...
"We walk by faith and not by sight"-2 Corinthians 5:7 Proverbs 3:5, 6 says, "Trust in The LORD with all thine heart; and lean not unto thine own understanding. In all thy ways acknowledge Him, and He shall direct thy paths."

No lack, But Abundance and Restoration...
Joel 2:25 says, "And I will restore to you the years that the locust hath eaten, the cankerworm, and the caterpillar, and the palmerworm..."

No fear, But Power and Boldness...
Isaiah 41:10 says, "Fear thou not; for I am with thee..."

No confusion, But Clarity and a Sound mind...
"For GOD hath not given us the spirit of fear; but of Power, and of Love, and of a Sound mind." 2 Timothy 1:7

No weariness, But Endurance and Strength...
Isaiah 40:31 says, "But they that wait upon the LORD shall renew their strength; they shall mount up with wings as eagles; they shall run, and not be weary; and they shall walk, and not faint."

No worries, But Peace and Hope...
Isaiah 26:3, one of my favorites says, *"Thou wilt keep him in perfect peace, who's mind is stayed on thee..."*
Isaiah 48:18 says, "O that thou hadst hearkened to My commandments! then had thy Peace been as a river, and thy righteousness as the waves of the sea."

"And let the peace of GOD rule in your hearts, to the which also ye are called in one body; and be ye thankful!"
Colossians 3:15

My Soul is Extremely is Prosperous

GOD has been and is, blessing me with extreme wealth in those things that many may not consider tangible in the natural. However has been a *ruby mine* in the spiritual.

"But lay up for yourselves treasures in heaven, where
neither moth nor rust doth corrupt, and where
thieves do not break through nor steal." Matthew 6:20

"...For a man's life consisteth not in the abundance of the
things which he possesseth." Luke 12:15

He is Prospering my spirit. Keeping it from being depleted, and adding to it in such a way, that it will maintain excellent health.

"Beloved, I wish above all things that thou mayest prosper
and be in health, even as thy soul prospereth." 3 John 1:2

In all of life conundrums we are but mere children who are forever trying to figure out what is, what is to be, and what is to come, and how that relates to ourselves and those that concerneth us. Moreover...What is the Perfect Will of GOD for our lives?

Along the Way...

We study the Word of GOD and, "We understand it better by and by." Only it's not the whole picture we want to grasp or define, but just a few feet ahead of us. I am learning that if we just trust and believe, knowing that GOD has our best interest in mind, bearing up to press on...we see breakthroughs and change... Circumstances rearrange! Trouble really doesn't last always. However it is in those trials that the most profitable and valuable education is obtained. Goes to show... no lessons are free. There is a price that someone had to pay for every valuable nugget of wisdom *along the way.*

"But as for you, ye thought evil against me; but God meant it unto good, to bring to pass, as it is this day, to save much people alive." Genesis 50:20

"How much better is it to get wisdom than gold! and to get understanding rather to be chosen silver!"
Proverbs 16:16

"...Wisdom is better than strength..." Ecclesiastes 9:16

GOD is so mindful of us. Over 7 billion people on this planet, and yet He knows the count of every hair on every head. WOW!!!

"But the very hairs of your head are all numbered."
Matthew 10:30

Peace

is the knowledge

trouble don't last always.

The understanding

all waves will cease to rage.

The assurance

loud roars will be hushed to a whisper

"There is Peace after the storm"

Along the Way...

"The Joy of the LORD is My Strength!"

2012... I delight in looking back over my life, the joyful times and the not so joyful times. It amazes me how through it all, GOD has allowed me, and given me the ability and strength to find contentment, even in times of extreme difficultly. GOD never ceases to amaze me! The Goodness of GOD is felt even in what we think are the most desert experiences. I truly thank GOD for that. Little things in life bring me joy. While we are to please GOD... Just the mention of Him pleases me so! Anytime that GOD allows us another day in the land of the living, not only does that mean our assignment on this earth is not completed, but it is a Tremendous Gift entrusted in us. That we will utilize what He placed inside of us. Doing everything *diminutively* miniscule, and *humongously deemed* valuable, unto the Glory of GOD. Knowing, everything we are or ever hope to be, is for GOD and His Ultimate Purpose. I believe when we truly understand that, it will help our vision not to be deterred...and our focus to be clearer.

While my desire is to do better and be better, GOD is enabling and fashioning me with a mindset to be strong and satisfied in the Process...Thank You LORD for continuing to strengthen me through Your Word and your Children... GOD knows what we need and when we need it.

#It's a Faith Walk

And we know, *"GOD is always working on our behalf..."* Even in the physical realm, when we do not feel a touch; a favorable and productive change; or see the harvest of what you've sowed. YET... He is working behind the dry walls of our natural sight. There are many intricate and crucial phases that are put in place in the building of a house...from the location to the foundation. And in reference to 'behind the dry wall.' There are many complex procedures that must take place in order for the house to stand and function properly for any duration of time. For example: Correct wiring, support beams, and insulation. (I will attempt to talk about this further in one of my new books that I am hoping will be completed by the end of 2014. GOD willing). I know a little about construction first hand. Daily I went to the construction site in which my house was being built, and I swept it clean. Understanding that the builders and I were a team. I brought them soda, water and sometimes food. When they left I tried to make sure I did what I could, to help the process in which the structure was being transformed and becoming what it was purposed to be. Such are we also under construction... Our heart, mind, soul, and all the inward parts. Those things about ourselves that we think are o.k. and we cannot see.

   He is also working on our environmental place of existence i.e. our atmosphere. Clearing out the rocks and debris in our life. There are atmospheric changes occurring in a dimension in time we know not of, that directly affects and relates to our particular situation and circumstances, that will cause alignment with the word and promises of GOD.

"For My thoughts are not your thoughts, neither are your ways My ways, saith the LORD. For as the heavens are higher than the earth, so are My ways higher than your ways, and My thoughts than your thoughts."
Isaiah 55:8, 9

"So shall My word be that goeth forth out of My mouth: it shall not return unto Me void, but it shall accomplish that which I please, and it shall prosper in the thing whereto I sent it."
Isaiah 55:11

Behind the Drywall and the scenes of our life, GOD is forever and continuously working it out for our GOoD. He will cause contentment and joy to spring forth... *"But Godliness with contentment is great gain."* 1 Timothy 6:6 knowing our steps are truly being ordered by the LORD... *The steps of a good man are ordered by the LORD: and he delighteth in His way. Psalm 37:23*

Allowing our focus and peace to come from doing and walking in His will and Purpose, He has set for our Lives. His Word is Truth. Who shall we believe? Adverse situations and circumstances, or the Word of GOD. I know I have reiterated several scriptures numerous times, however they possess so much wealth, it merits me to do so. With that said, Always remember *Romans 8:28... "And we know that all things work together for good to them that love GOD, to them who are the called according to His Purpose."*

If GOD has parted your "Red Sea"...
Don't be afraid to walk through it.
He won't let the rushing winds, or the gushing waves
collapse or over take you...

If it appears that you missed your opportunity to go through
to get to... the other side...
and the sea has lost its divide...
swim across it anyhow...
You won't drown or be consumed.
GOD won't let you down.
You must begin to see yourself on the other side.

Not being in the place and purpose that
GOD has called you to be
is living in bondage...
GOD'S intentions are for you to be free.
And all that He Predestined you to be.
"To much is given, much is required..."
Don't stay in the wilderness
too long...

Know that GOD has much more for you, and when you are obedient, His love and Gifts will flow through you to help others...You say you like to Bless, than get into position for GOD to Bless you...so you can Bless others. Don't miss your season. Who is depending on you?
Again I tell you
Don't look at the Raging Sea...
Only Believe

Along the Way...

> *"And the LORD answered me, and said, Write the vision, and make it plain upon tables, that he may run that readeth it."*
> Habakkuk 2: 2

Many of you have already realized and recognized, that talents and gifts were placed in each and every one of you, to be multiplied. And like many, I don't think there is a day that goes by that I don't have a new idea, invention, alteration to an existing product on the market, book or movie concept, and or a new business venture, etc. Oftentimes I'm sleeping when inspiration presents itself, so I wake up writing. [I hope you don't mind, but I think this is a good time to interject an amusing excerpt of dialogue] I was telling my children last year... "I am literally sitting on Billions of dollars."... My daughter replied with a *rhythmic lag,* as if she was singing a song...excitedly, but respectfully with a slight smile... "Well Mommy get up."...

If you have many ideas and you want to see it manifest, not allowing your gifts that GOD put in you to lie dormant; but instead for them to manifest & multiply for the Glory of GOD, allowing you another stream. With every idea GOD gives us, He is giving us increase...When we "get up" and work what GOD has deposited in us. I believe if we do what we can, in whatever capacity we have to do it in, GOD will make opportunities to get it done, and to multiply and prosper...Creating dividends and a harvest to give back. Everyday make some type of effort towards your goals. I once heard someone say, "Pray as though everything depends on GOD & work as though everything depends on you. #manifestyourdreams NOW!

"But Seek Ye first the Kingdom of GOD, and His righteousness; and all these things shall be added unto you."

Matthew 6:33

Along the Way...

Pursuit of Happiness....

What I've learned....
While we are pursuing "things", (anything we "think" might add or make us happy) and trying to walk in our GOD given purpose...We can be content on the journey before we arrive... That way, when we reach are destination, not only are we whole and complete, but we are grateful and satisfied that, *along the way* we took time out to enjoy, learn and embrace. We can help and tell someone else how to ride it out in peace.

Although the journey forever continues,
I believe there are pivotal times and areas of completion...
Seasons of test and semester completed.
Life is definitely a classroom,
and I am a student... Forever learning, and I am grateful...
While I may not always like the learning process (tears of joy and sadness) and some of the choices I have made *along the way* that made the Lessons tougher ...
I am so Thankful to GOD... For His Grace, His Mercy,
His Loving Kindness that make life's Journey
not only bearable,
but sweet...
Matthew 11:30 Says, *"For my yoke is easy, and my burden is light."*

> *"I know both how to be abased, and I know how to abound: every where and in all things I am instructed both to be full and to be hungry, both to abound and to suffer need."*
> *Philippians 4:12*

Throughout my life I've always had great expectations and huge aspirations. However life's events happened, and instead of me affecting the flow, I sometimes went with the currents, while keeping my raft somewhat intact. Although it's harder to paddle against the tides… that is what it takes for a shifting to occur. I used to put off the pursuit of my dearest dreams and endeavors, anticipating a *sooner* calmness, waiting for a more favorable time with fewer difficult and more desirable circumstances. Then as time went on, the years progressed, I got younger *(smile)* and things didn't get easier, or become "ideal". It even seemed as though trials began to escalate in their effort to *up the ante* in belligerence and chaos.

Ironically after all the years of trying to maneuver through a maze of uncertainties, and waiting for things to get better… At a most tumultuous time. I began the process of *Going to Work with one shoe*. A phase I conceptualized and coined after seeing one of my favorite movies… "The Pursuit of Happyness". I began to finally press through to a more fullness of my purpose, during a period in my life that seemed extreme to me…

Along the Way...

My Greatest time of difficulties led to my Greatest Blessings, Breakthroughs and Triumphs. I've been through more than I care to elaborate on. However, through it all GOD kept me intact; mentally, Spiritually, and restored me physically! A divorced lady, who lost her job, home, car totaled, and was in almost constant pain for months, from the injuries sustained in a car wreck. (Now this perspective of pain is coming from a woman who experienced 15 hours of natural labor...) Let me add...in an extreme financial deficit i.e. no money, no computer and in somewhat of an obscure place of abandonment...and yes there are some *etcetera, etcetera's...*

I'm glad I had a heart to see...
and a mind to hear other's need...
When an opportunity was presented to me.
Never ignoring someone else's plight.
GOD gives us all sight
to be sensitive to those around us.
Sacrificially.

My greatest deficit lead to my most Incredible deposit.
*"For your shame ye shall have double; and for confusion they shall rejoice in their portion: therefore in their land they shall possess the double: **everlasting joy shall be unto them**."*
Isaiah 61:7

After the LORD healed me... I never will forget my first long walk, it was to Staples Office Supply. I needed to print a copy of my manuscript so that I could edit and rectify any typographical errors that night, since I didn't have a computer. (So please forgive my "*typos*"... *One woman show*)

The walk was fine, however trying to get across the busy road was and obstacle course. Nevertheless I made it! I prayed all the way there, and repeated, "I am healed in JESUS Mighty Name! Thank You LORD!!!!"

After being partially immobile for months, I was so happy and elated, and I felt a humungous sense of accomplishment! I think I will be back to jogging again real soon!

...And your 'real soon' is coming too, if you have the courage to believe and try... for the first time or *again;* pursuing your purpose and dreams on this earth...Always remember, if and when things get tougher, in your effort and Pursuit, take it as a sign and a blessing that Better days are on the way... I.e. The process has begun...

Seeing a Glimpse of Purpose and Destiny
...you can either hurt through the process or focus on the preparation with somewhat patient expectancy...

Preparing is part of the process of Pursuit.

Whenever there is Opposition, know that there is a Position waiting for you to occupy. When others say you can't, say you can. When others say you won't, say you will.

In the words of *Nike*... **"Just Do It!"** *and I add* **Anyhow!**

Along the Way...

I decided to "Run On…"
I made it over the first hurdle. I saw many more that I needed to jump and get over… Nevertheless… Guided by the LORD…I would concentrate on one at a time. Sometimes I paced myself, because I didn't always have the strength and emotional stamina. There were times I had to limp and there were times I ran…But I knew I had to press towards the finish line…Yes maybe all the by- standers had gone home, and they deemed me as lost and least, without a cause and vision and ability to see what was in front of me…They thought it was over for me… and they thought I wouldn't make it. So maybe there was no one left to cheer me on, and the crowd had gone… I felt alone, tired and worn…But GOD was there to edge me on. He continued to increase my strength. "The more I pressed, the more His Supernatural pushed me." I ran and jumped while He used a few that remained to maneuver me through the course. Elated and relieved because it had been so long since I had achieved. I felt a sense of accomplishment in my spirit. Preparing, sprinting and gaining momentum to go on to the next hurdle, running harder and encouraging myself as well, "I can't give up now"…As I approached the next 7 hurdles… Miraculously every single one lifted out of my way in mid-air. The finish line was before me, and to my surprise there were many there praying for me. I said at the beginning of this year that I was going to run a Marathon… and run a Marathon I did…Now I am "running on to see what the ends gonna be." I do not think I'm late, delayed, or behind… I Believe… I am right on Time!!! When I saw a Glimpse of my Purpose and Destiny I decided not to hurt through the process or give in…But instead to press and to pray for GOD to enable me to begin again. I see Victory in sight. Courage beat fear and enabled me to WIN!!!! We are ALL Winners if we Believe and try again…

Oftentimes I wonder in Overwhelming gratitude…Why does GOD Bless us so much? And then I think about how He loves us just that much!!! He wants us to have an abundant life full of His Goodness and His Promises, and that we experience and recognize His Agape Love daily.

"For God so loved the world, that He gave His only begotten Son, that whosoever believeth in Him should not perish, but have everlasting life." John 3:16

It is not GOD'S Will that any of us should perish.

"The Lord is not slack concerning his promise, as some men count slackness; but is longsuffering to us-ward, not willing that any should perish, but that all should come to repentance." 2 Peter 3:9

"If we confess our sins, He is faithful and just to forgive us our sins, and to cleanse us from all unrighteousness." 1 John 1:9

The MOST Important step in ensuring a future is to make your election sure. GOD Loves you Unconditionally, Perfectly and Endlessly! Love Him back. Come as you are. Confess Him as LORD over your life. Ask Him for forgiveness in the pardons of your sins… By faith Believe and Receive! And allow His perfect work to take place in your heart. Be obedient and strive to please Him…
#POSSIBLE

Along the Way...

"That if thou shalt confess with thy mouth the LORD JESUS, and shalt believe in thine heart that GOD hath raised Him from the dead, thou shalt be saved. For with the heart man believeth unto righteousness; and with the mouth confession is made unto salvation."
Romans 10:9-10

"Behold, I stand at the door, and knock: If any man hear My voice, and open the door, I will come in to him, and will sup with him, and him with Me."
Revelation 3:20

"Then spake JESUS again unto them, saying, I am the light of the world: he that followeth Me shall not walk in darkness, but shall have the light of life."
John 8:12

"Therefore if any man be in CHRIST, he is a new creature: old things are passed away; behold, all things are become new."
2 Corinthians 5:17

*"...Thou shalt love the LORD thy GOD
with all thy heart, and with all thy soul,
and with all thy strength, and with all thy mind;
and thy neighbor as thyself."
Luke 10:27*

Along the Way...

Love is Priceless

Giving from the Heart cost nothing...
But has more value than silver or gold
And is the wealthiest place
to give and receive from...

One act of kindness, one gesture of love,
one smile
one word of encouragement, one hug
could mean everything and change a life forever...
We really never know what people are going through.
You can't tell by the way they dress, their facade
or by the way they seem to have it all together.
We really don't know how much of a difference
your existence
on this earth and in someone else's life could mean
to another human being.
Sometimes your light, your smile,
your heartache, your strength through it all,
is not just to enlighten and show you the way...
but the ones that are watching...
Let your love and your light shine...
Even through your trials

May be you won't do something for every human being
but you can start with one...
Take advantage of the opportunities that GOD gives you
to make a difference on this earth...
Someway, Somehow
Start today

Along the Way...

What if almost every single human on this earth, looked after or cared for someone else (they didn't know) Along the Way? An act of kindness, a little help, or a hand up, goes along way... just to know another human being cares... will make lighter the burdens that they bear...

Over the years seeing the humungous work that has been done by the many charitable organizations in the earth...We are one that is attempting to be of help as well, by continuing to contribute to some of those various organizations in existence, to help undergird, serve, and add in some way to the work that has already started, we pray.

10% of Proceeds from the sales of all Along the Way Books and other selected Products will go to the development, establishing and maintaining **Be A Blessing- Along the Way Non-Profit** *An organization that is in Great Expectation and Anticipation of being a Blessing to many, Along the Way...*

It's so wonderful to know that GOD is not done... Loving you, taking care of you, watching over you, protecting you, comforting you, and Blessing you...

Along the Way Journal, Devotional and Other Products coming soon! **Thank GOD for the Rhythm in our Hearts...** *Blessings!*

Gleaning Handfuls of Purpose
Along the Way…

There is So Much more I want to convey…

However that would take me forever and a decade…

So for now I will call it a day…

I will be writing for you soon,

Again I Say and I pray

That you would experience and notice

GOD'S Many Blessings

Along the Way…

~Lynda~

"Still holding on to His hands…"

GOD Loves You!!!!

www.ingramcontent.com/pod-product-compliance
Lightning Source LLC
LaVergne TN
LVHW091302080426
835510LV00007B/362